To Mum
&
Bi...

...004,
...Stuart
...otte.
x

Steve

MELBOURNE

Moments in a day

Melbourne Moments
30

31

Sunrise

Morning's first rays gleam on the water.

The day emerges gently from Melbourne's mist

Warming Up

BSL
brother
Westpac
650 2054
RIVER
MV YARRA DUCHESS

Mid-morning light falls on the city and the Yarra River.

Lush gardens and tranquil waterways sit well
with urban metal and stone.

The banks of the Yarra are a wonderful place to take in the morning - or just sleep in the sun.

Port Phillip Bay is perfect for fishing or just taking in the fresh sea air.

NEPEAN

Noon

Places to meet, play and be entertained.

Meeting and eating: there are many options for lunch.

Melbourne's markets and merchants
and a midday coffee break.

Luna Park
IN MELBOURNE
New Luna Park
RIDE ALL DAY
from $22.95
OPERATING HOURS
SCHOOL HOLIDAYS*
PUBLIC HOLIDAYS*

Colour and art enliven the streets.

Melbourne's history and future are
reflected in her elegant architecture.

above Market bargains and café culture.

right Stopping for a chat.

16
UNIVERSITY
852

Melbourne's much-loved trams.

In the streets, in the park, on the water or by the bay;
making the most of the fine weather.

RR 159

In Melbourne, sport is not a pastime;
it's a passion.

SPICERS PAPER
ANSETT

It's easy to spend the afternoon in a garden haven,
hidden away amidst the city's hustle and bustle.

Bright bursts of colour in Melbourne's
beautiful flower gardens.

Winding Down

Taking an afternoon break in bayside St Kilda.

Like a row of brightly coloured sweets,
Victorian-era bathing boxes line Brighton beach.

Shadows lengthen in the afternoon sun.

The sun might be setting but Melbourne
continues to work and play.

Cosy cafés and pubs are inviting on a grey afternoon.

THE FITZ cafe
Wine & Beer Shop

Sunset

above Water magic and colour brighten the night.

right Memory is eternal at the Shrine of Remembrance.

食為先酒樓
SAWASDEE
CHEMIST
CHINATOWN
CAR PARK

An evening glow lights Melbourne's streets.

Melbourne illuminated by nature and lights at night.

Index

Note: For multiple-image pages, locations are listed in a clockwise direction from top left.

Cover Melbourne tram, St Kilda.

2-3 Brighton.

4-6 Port Phillip Bay, Geelong.

7 Rowers on the Yarra River.

8 Yarra River; Melbourne skyline and St Kilda Rd; Princes Walk.

9 Yarra River shrouded in mist.

10-11 Princes Bridge viewed from Alexandra Gardens.

12 CBD viewed from Southbank.

13 Yarra River and CBD.

14 Architectural detail; Capital City Trail, Southbank; Royal Botanic Gardens; tram.

15 Swans on the Yarra River.

16 Capital City Trail and the Yarra River.

17 Royal Botanic, Fitzroy, Queen Victoria, and Alexandra Gardens.

18 Williamstown.

19 Queenscliff.

20-21 Carlton Gardens and CBD.

22 Crown Entertainment Complex.

23 Yarra Promenade; Southgate; Princes Bridge.

24 Acland St, St Kilda; Southgate; Chapel St, Prahran; Southgate; Lygon St, Carlton.

25 Swanston St.

26-27 Acland St, St Kilda.

28 Luna Park, St Kilda.

29 Mosaic mural detail; *Ophelia* by Deborah Halpern, Southgate; tram pole detail, Swanston St.

30-31 Colonial architecture.

32 Market and cafés, Brunswick St, Fitzroy.

33 Queen Victoria Market.

34 St Kilda.

35 Various trams.

36 Flinders St; Williamstown Foreshore; Acland St, St Kilda; The Esplanade, St Kilda.

37 On the banks of the Yarra River.

38 Melbourne Cricket Ground; Flemington Racecourse; Albert Park.

39 Australian Rules Football.

40 Royal Exhibition Building, Carlton.

41 Royal Botanic Gardens (top left and centre); Queen Victoria Gardens; Royal Melbourne Zoo; Royal Botanic Gardens.

42-43 Carlton Gardens.

44-45 Port Phillip Bay.

46-47 St Kilda.

48-49 Brighton.

50 Southbank Promenade.

51 Parliament House; The Esplanade, St Kilda; Royal Botanic Gardens.

52 Melbourne skyline; Collins St; St Kilda; Flinders St.

53 Victorian Arts Centre

54 Fitzroy; Fitzroy; St Kilda.

55 Brunswick St, Fitzroy.

56-57 West Gate Bridge.

58 Southbank; Princess Theatre.

59 Shrine of Remembrance.

60 Little Bourke St, Chinatown.

61 Lygon St, Carlton; Collins St; Lygon St.

62 Melbourne skyline.

63 Theatre Building, Victorian Arts Centre; Flinders Street Station; Crown Towers Hotel viewed across the Yarra River; St Pauls Cathedral.

Back Cover Flinders Street Station.